CHURCH

CHURCH IN WILLOUGHBY

EATING
THE LORD

WITNESS LEE

Living Stream Ministry
Anaheim, CA

First Edition, September 2000.

ISBN 0-7363-1036-3

Published by

Living Stream Ministry
2431 W. La Palma Ave., Anaheim, CA 92801 U.S.A.
P. O. Box 2121, Anaheim, CA 92814 U.S.A.

Printed in the United States of America

00 01 02 03 04 05 / 9 8 7 6 5 4 3 2 1

CONTENTS

PREFACE

This book is a translation of messages given by Brother Witness Lee, which were published in Chinese in September 1979. This translation was not reviewed by the speaker.

CHAPTER ONE

THE BIBLE BEING A BOOK OF EATING

Scripture Reading: Gen. 2:8-9, 16; Exo. 12:6-8; Deut. 12:6-7; 15:19-20; 16:10-11, 15; John 6:35, 57, 63; Rev. 22:2, 14

THE BIBLE—A BOOK OF EATING

The Bible is a wonderful book. What does the Bible speak about? It is entirely correct for us to say that the Bible speaks about Christ, life, and salvation. Moreover, it is not wrong to say that the Bible speaks about wives submitting to their husbands, husbands loving their wives, children honoring their parents, and parents caring for their children. Neither is it wrong to say that the Bible speaks about humility, patience, peace, and goodness. Nor is it wrong to say that it speaks about God's love, God's light, and God's holiness. Furthermore, it is not wrong to say that the Bible teaches us to worship God, to love God, and to serve God. We can list hundreds and even thousands of topics that the Bible speaks about. However, the strange thing is that we may never have heard a message in Christianity telling us that the Bible speaks about eating.

It is true that the Bible is a book of life, a book of salvation, a book of love, and a book of teachings. However, after reading the Scripture verses above, you have to admit that the Bible is a book on eating.

After God created man, God did not say that man needed life or salvation. Neither did He say that man needed to love and obey God. Nor did He say that man needed to be humble or to be peaceable. After God created man, He put man in a garden, and He placed man before the tree of life, telling him in effect, "Eat! Eat! Eat!" What does the Bible speak about?

It speaks about eating. What kind of book is the Bible? It is a book on eating.

The Bible is a profound and mysterious book. It does not become boring even after repeated readings, and it cannot be exhausted even after you have read it a hundred times, a thousand times, or ten thousand times. Regardless of how many times you read the Bible, there are still new things. Thirty years ago I already had worn out three or four Bibles from repeatedly reading them, and I thought I understood the Bible almost completely. However, I gradually came to realize that there are still many truths in the Bible that I have not seen. At this time if you were to ask me, "Brother Lee, what have you now uncovered from the Bible?" I would say, "Now I have uncovered one word—eat."

READING THE BIBLE REQUIRING US
TO DROP OUR OLD CONCEPTS

Brothers and sisters, this word is clearly in the Bible, yet we did not see it even after reading the Bible many times. Why? It is because every old concept we have is a veil. It is more than evident that the word *eat* is in the Bible, yet we could not see it. This is due to the fact that we have our old preconceived notions, our old concepts.

The verses in the Scripture reading from the book of Deuteronomy contain a statement that is repeated many times: "You shall eat,...you and your households" (12:7). Yet we may not see this even after numerous times of reading. However, when we read Joshua 24, we clearly see a sentence such as, "As for me and my house, we will serve Jehovah" (v. 15). This sentence is spoken only once in the sixty-six books in the Bible, but every Christian sees it. Why? This is because our natural concept is to serve God; we simply do not have the concept of eating the Lord. Therefore, even after having read the verses on this subject a thousand times, we still may not see the word *eat*. Eating is in the Bible, but it is not in your concept. Instead, the word *serve* is in your concept. Honestly speaking, even without Joshua 24, according to your mentality you would always say, "I and my household will serve Jehovah." It just so happens that the

Bible has such a verse that corresponds with your concept. Therefore, the idea is quickly imprinted in your mind immediately after you have read the verse. This is not to read the Bible into your mind; rather, it is to read your mind into the Bible. This is our problem with respect to reading the Bible.

God says that His thoughts are not our thoughts, yet we are not willing to drop our thoughts. Every time you come to read the Bible, you are not actually reading the Bible; you are reading your concept. For example, day after day you have the concept that wives should submit to their husbands and that husbands should love their wives. Therefore, one day when you come to Ephesians 5 concerning wives submitting to their husbands and husbands loving their wives, you are quick to see this. However, you may not see the many more important words in the Bible, even though you have read them again and again.

GENESIS—GOD'S DESIRE BEING
FOR MAN TO EAT THE TREE OF LIFE

What does the Bible speak about from beginning to end? All those who know the Bible acknowledge that there is a principle in the Bible: The way a certain thing is spoken of the first time in the Bible record becomes the immutable meaning of that thing in its later development. Therefore, if we want to know the proper relationship between God and man, we have to see what God wanted man to do after He created him. After God created Adam, He did not say, "Adam, I created you. I am your Lord. You have to worship Me, and you have to thank and praise Me." We do not see these words recorded in the Bible. These thoughts are man's religious concepts. I am not suggesting that these concepts are bad, but these religious concepts came out of man's fallen thoughts. They were not the thought in the beginning. After Adam was created, God placed him in front of the tree of life and told him to freely eat of the fruit of the trees in the garden. The first thing God wanted man to do was to eat, eat, and eat! Therefore, we see that the Bible is a book on eating. To eat what? Eat God! Eat the Lord!

However, you can see that man immediately made a mistake

in what he ate, and he fell. It is dreadful to eat the wrong thing. Adam fell because he ate the wrong thing. Our physical eating is a symbol of this matter. Anything we eat, whether it is of the animal life or the plant life, gives us the life supply. If we eat the wrong thing, we can be poisoned. In some cases we can become sick, but in the more serious cases we can die. The same is true in the spiritual realm. Only God is the right food; it is right for us to eat God only. If we eat anything other than God, we eat the wrong thing. Not surprisingly, every human being has been poisoned. The last sentence in Genesis says, "They embalmed him, and he was put in a coffin in Egypt" (50:26). This was the end of Joseph, and it is the end of the entire human race as well. This is the outcome of the man who was created by God and who was poisoned. After being poisoned, man died; after his death, he was placed in a coffin; after being placed in a coffin, he remained in Egypt.

EXODUS—GOD'S DESIRE
BEING FOR MAN TO EAT THE LAMB

After the book of Genesis, there is Exodus. In Exodus God came to save the man who was still in Egypt. How did God carry out His salvation? This time God presented Himself in another form. In Genesis God had presented Himself as the tree of life; in Exodus God presented Himself as the Lamb.

First God presented Himself as a plant; then He presented Himself as an animal. Both are not enormously big figures. A lamb is small. I believe the tree of life was neither a big tree nor a tall tree that would be out of Adam's reach. In fact, I believe that the tree of life was not a tree that grew upward but a tree that grew by spreading out like a vine. Therefore, God did not present Himself as something truly great.

I am not saying that God is not great; however, when the great God gave Himself to us to be eaten by us, He reduced Himself. When Jesus came the first time, the Jews were waiting for a Messiah. In their concept the Messiah had to be a great One. However, when the Lord Jesus came, they looked at Him and found Him to be One who appeared weak, without attracting form or majesty, and who was born in the city of Nazareth in Galilee. He was indeed very small.

One day this small Jesus performed something spectacular. He fed five thousand people, not counting the women and children, with five loaves and two fish. Therefore, the Jews said, "This is the Prophet! Come, let us make Him King." The Lord Jesus quickly fled when He heard this. Do not applaud Him; if you do, He will not receive it. If you put Him in a high position, He will not accept it; rather, He will run away. On the next day the Lord Jesus came back not in a way to show off His strength and power but in a hidden way. He came back and said in effect, "I am the bread of life. I come to be your food. I have no intention to be your King. Do not worship Me. The more you worship Me, the more I am displeased with you. If you eat Me, I am happy. I am the bread of life; he who eats Me shall live because of Me."

This is neither a moral concept nor a religious concept; it is truly a divine concept. To this day we still have our religious concepts; we still have the feeling that the Lord is high above in heaven and that He is altogether holy. I am not saying that this concept is wrong or that it is not good. What I am saying is that this concept is not God's concept. God's concept is not for you to do anything except to eat Him.

CHRIST COMING FOR US TO EAT

The verses we read in Deuteronomy 15 say that the first-born ox should not be put to work and the firstborn sheep should not be shorn; instead, they should be eaten (vv. 19-20). What does this mean according to typology? When many Christians and non-Christians talk about Christ, they expect that Christ will either till the ground or be shorn. No one thinks of eating Christ. To ask Christ to till the ground means to ask Him to labor on your behalf, to do things for you. Did you know that every day you want the Lord Jesus to till the ground for you? You do not have a way to deal with your wife, so you pray, "Lord, You know the kind of wife You have given me; I am helpless. Please deal with her." This is to ask the Lord Jesus to till the ground for you. Some sisters may pray, "Lord, You know how stubborn my husband is. Lord, You have to deal with him; otherwise, I will not be able to bear it any longer." When you ask the Lord to do things for you in this way, you are asking Him to till the ground as an ox.

What is the meaning of shearing the sheep of the wool? Wool is used to make clothing. You may want Christ to be your outward adornment; you try to imitate Christ outwardly. It is rare to find Christians who have escaped these two things. Those Christians who do not love the Lord simply ignore Him. However, Christians who love the Lord want Him either to till the ground or to be shorn.

The Bible does not tell us to till the ground but to eat. Do not ask Christ to do anything for you; rather, eat Christ into you. Do not pray and ask Christ to change your wife; instead, eat Christ into you and live by Him! Your wife may not change a bit; yet to you, to live is Christ. Do not ask the Lord to give your husband a beating; the Lord will never answer this kind of prayer. The Lord will say, "I will use My staff as a whip to beat you instead." You have to eat the Lord. When you eat the Lord, any mistreatment from your husband will be sweet to you. Hallelujah! You do not need the Lord to till the ground; neither do you need to shear Him. You simply need to eat Him.

It seems that the Lord is saying, "I am the bread of life. He who eats Me shall live because of Me. Do not expect Me to do anything for you or expect Me to be your outward adornment. You have to understand that I come to give you life and to give it more abundantly. I want to enter into you to be your life and your everything. As long as I live in you, you should not care about the outward circumstances. It is good if your wife has changed; it is even better if she has not changed. It is good to have a submissive wife; it is even better to have an unsubmissive wife. A warm and tender husband is lovely, of course; however, a rough and tough husband is even lovelier."

Therefore, what matters today is to have life within us, not to implore Christ to do anything for us. As long as Christ enters into us to be our life and our supply, we can do the things that others cannot do, we can endure the sufferings that others cannot endure, and we can bear the burdens that others cannot bear. Do not till the ground or shear the sheep. Instead, eat the Lord! Do not expect Him to be your Prophet or your King. He came to be the bread of life to you. There-fore, eat Him!

Brothers and sisters, what does the Bible speak about? Eating! For what reason did Jesus come? He came for us to eat Him. Whenever fundamental Christianity speaks about the Feast of Passover, the blood of the lamb is invariably regarded with utmost importance. I am not suggesting that the blood is not important. Man sinned, and he needs the blood. In the Garden of Eden, however, there was the tree of life; there was no blood. It was when man sinned that the blood was needed, but the lamb has not only blood but also flesh. The blood deals with our sins due to our fall, and the flesh supplies us with the life from the tree of life. Hence, it is not only the blood; it is the blood with the flesh.

When you read Exodus 12, you can see these two things—the blood and the flesh. The blood was sprinkled outside the house, so the house was under the blood. What were the children of Israel doing under the covering of the blood? They were eating. Many in Christianity speak clearly about the blood, but the focus of the Passover lamb is not on the blood but on the flesh. The blood is for the flesh; the sprinkling of the blood is for man to eat the flesh. The blood is for redemption, and redemption is to bring man back to the enjoyment of Christ as life.

DEUTERONOMY—GOD'S DESIRE BEING FOR MAN TO EAT THE PRODUCE OF CANAAN

In the book of Deuteronomy, you see all kinds of produce as different kinds of offerings for the people of Israel to bring before God. These different kinds of produce are all types of Christ. Although the offerings are for God, eventually they are for us to eat. We offer them to God, yet they become our food. Therefore, we must eat what we offer.

At this stage, what we enjoy is not only the lamb but also a feast. In this feast we have oxen, sheep, pigeons, grain, new wine, and all kinds of firstfruits. We have a rich feast that includes both plants and animals. Furthermore, we eat this feast not only once; we eat it for seven days. In all seven days of the Feast, we eat a feast every day.

Today we eat Christ not only as the tree of life and as the Lamb but also as a feast. We are keeping the Feast of Christ. Every church meeting is to keep the feast and eat Christ. Come and keep the feast! Come and eat Christ!

REVELATION—GOD'S DESIRE STILL BEING FOR MAN TO EAT THE TREE OF LIFE

Finally, at the end of Revelation you see the New Jerusalem with a river of water and the tree of life growing on both sides of the river. There is a verse in the last chapter of Revelation that says, "Blessed are those who wash their robes that they may have right to the tree of life" (v. 14). Therefore, we see that eating and drinking the Lord is our destiny. This is God's ordination. If you do anything else or have any other choice, you will find death. God's ordination is our destiny. We should not have our own choice.

God ordained even before the foundation of the world that our destiny, our future, would be to daily eat the Lord. What must Christians do? Eat the Lord! What kind of Christian are you? We are Christians who eat the Lord. What kind of church do you have? A church that eats the Lord. Christians are people who eat the Lord. This is the Lord's recovery. What is the Lord recovering? The Lord is recovering the matter of eating Him. Christianity in general has lost the matter of eating the Lord, and it has lost sight of the fact that believers have the right to eat the Lord. The Lord is recovering this today.

Blessed are those who have washed their robes because they have the right to the tree of life. It is not the right to worship and to serve but the right to eat. Recently when the church in Los Angeles has met, the chairs were not neatly arranged in single rows but rather in many small circles. I have heard that they plan to set up small round tables, so that they can sit around them during meetings to enjoy the feast. This is very meaningful. Consider the way the benches are arranged in this meeting hall. When the brothers and sisters come together and occupy the benches row by row, it looks like a "Sunday worship service." When you are seated in this way, the atmosphere of Sunday worship is present. Do not think that the seating arrangement does not deserve consideration. When everyone is seated in this orderly way, this is religion, and the atmosphere of eating is gone. But to have small round tables here, each with five or six chairs, and to sit around them gives the atmosphere of feasting.

THE WAY TO EAT

The Lord whom we eat as our food is the Spirit. Therefore, which organ do we use to eat Him? We use our spirit to eat Him. The Lord is Spirit, so we must use our spirit to eat Him. How do we eat Him? By calling, "O Lord! O Lord!" To call on the Lord is to eat Him. The Bible clearly shows us that the Lord is our food, and we must eat Him. As the Spirit He is our food. The organ by which we eat Him is also the spirit. Moreover, the way to eat Him is by calling on the Lord's name. Calling on the Lord is eating the Lord.

Some may say that we do not appear to be holding a Sunday worship service with our calling and shouting. They are absolutely right. We do not care for their kind of Sunday worship; we come here to eat the Lord. How do we eat? By calling on the Lord. You can be refined in many other gatherings but not in a time of eating. Calling on the Lord's name may not be considered refined, but I know it is truly sweet, because I have tasted it. We thank and praise the Lord that this is the Lord's recovery today! What is the Lord recovering? Eating the Lord! Hallelujah!

CHAPTER TWO

THE LORD BEING FOR MAN TO EAT

Scripture Reading: Matt 15:21-28; Luke 14:15-16; 15:22-24; 1 Cor. 3:2; 1 Pet. 2:2

READING THE BIBLE TO TOUCH THE LIFE IN IT

The Bible is an extraordinary book. The concepts and points of emphasis in the Bible are often beyond what we can think and are even contrary to our natural concepts. Therefore, whenever we come to the Bible, we have to learn to completely drop our own concepts. When we read the Bible, we need to say to the Lord from our innermost being, "Lord, get rid of my concepts; remove my veils that I may see the pure light in Your Word and touch the pure feelings in You."

Many of us have read the New Testament many times. I believe that in your reading you have picked up many teachings from the Bible. However, if you examine them closely, you will discover that most of them are concepts that already existed in your mind. We can almost say that you cannot get any concept out of your reading of the Bible unless that concept was already there in your mind.

Why is it that we often read the Bible as if it were a book on ethics and morality? This is because ethics and morality are in our concepts. Why is it that when we read the Bible, all we can see is that we need to serve the Lord, to labor for the Lord, to be zealous for the Lord, and to do this or that for the Lord? This also is because these notions already exist in us. Therefore, it is easy to see these items when we read the Bible.

I would like to say, yes, all these ethical concepts, moral concepts, and concepts such as serving the Lord and laboring for the Lord exist in the Bible. These items are found in the Bible, but they are the issues of the life that is in the Bible. This may be likened to a pot of flowers. They have their outward appearance, shape, and color. However, their outward shape and color are not something only external; they are the growth and expression of the life within the flowers. Every kind of life has the essence, the power, and the shape of that life. If you allow this life to develop, its shape and outward appearance will become manifested. Therefore, the outward appearance is the expression of the life within.

Today when we read the Bible, it is very easy for us to see the outward appearance and the shape, but it is not easy for us to touch the life within. This is the fundamental difficulty in our reading of the Bible. Now how do we see the life within the Bible? Simply put, it is in the matter of eating.

THE LORD BEING THE CHILDREN'S BREAD
FOR MAN TO EAT

Let us use an illustration. Matthew 15 speaks about the Lord leaving the land of Judea and withdrawing to the Gentile region of Tyre and Sidon. A Canaanite woman came forward and cried, "Have mercy on me, Lord, Son of David! My daughter suffers terribly from demon possession" (v. 22). Although she was a Gentile woman, she addressed the Lord Jesus as the Son of David according to the traditional concept of Judaism. However, the Lord replied, "It is not good to take the children's bread and throw it to the little dogs" (v. 26). The woman used the religious title "Son of David"; Jesus' answer was concerning a piece of bread. What a vast difference between the words they said to each other!

The Son of David as a royal descendant and an Heir to the throne was a great man. In man's religious concept Christ was considered an incredibly great man and the Heir in the royal family. However, Jesus' reply was that He was the children's bread. Now let me ask you, "Who is greater, the Son of David or the children?" Everyone will agree that the Son of David is greater. Now let me ask you another question, "Which is greater, the children or the children's bread?" Needless to say, the children are greater than the children's bread.

Therefore, consider this: Who is greater, you or the Lord
Jesus? You have to boldly say, "I am greater because I am a
child, and He is the bread." However, you would dare not
declare that you are greater because of the influence of the
traditional concepts in religion. To say that we are greater
than the Lord is not a blasphemy to the Lord but a genuine
knowing of the Lord. With all sincerity of heart, you can say,
"Lord, I thank You and praise You! Today You have become
my food. The eater is always greater than the food. Lord, You
have become the small food for me to eat!"

When the Lord Jesus withdrew to Tyre and Sidon, there
appeared a Canaanite woman who was pitiful, lowly, and
base. She regarded the Lord Jesus as the Son of David, a
descendant of the royal household. However, the Lord was
wise, and His response was wonderful—simple but profound.
He said, "It is not good to take the children's bread and throw
it to the little dogs." He wanted the Canaanite woman to
know this: "If I were the Son of David, I would not have come
to you. The Son of David should be on the throne, not in
Tyre and Sidon. You have to know that I am the children's
bread. You have to also know your position. If I were the Son
of David, you would not be qualified to cry out to Me. If I were
the children's bread, you would neither be qualified to eat
Me. You are a Gentile dog. You do not know Me thoroughly,
nor do you know yourself accurately."

The Lord was truly wise, and the meaning of His answer
was truly profound. Nevertheless, on that day the Holy Spirit
worked in the Canaanite woman so that her understanding
was opened immediately after hearing the Lord's word. She
did not argue or get angry. It is as if she said, "Lord, You are
right. You are the children's bread, and I am a heathen dog.
However, You have to know that even dogs have their portion.
The dogs' portion is not on the table but under the table. The
dogs cannot eat the bread on the table, but shouldn't the
crumbs under the table be their portion?" The response of this
Canaanite woman was also very meaningful. It is tantamount
to saying, "Lord, You have to know that even though You are
the children's bread, the bread is not on the table anymore
because Your naughty children have dropped You off the

table. As a heathen dog, I am under the table, but You are also under the table. I am in Tyre and Sidon, but You are also not in Jerusalem. Hence, You are now my portion."

THE LORD BECOMING SMALL ENOUGH
TO ENTER INTO US

Brothers and sisters, you have to see the significance of this case. People invariably address the Lord Jesus according to their religious concepts, regarding Him as a great man. However, the Lord clearly reveals to us that He is not so. We have to know the Lord not according to the religious concept but according to the revelation in His Word. Today, the whole world sees Christ in the same way as the Canaanite woman did. Therefore, some say that Christ was a religious teacher, others say that Christ was the founder of a religion, and still others say that Christ was a great man. These are what the unbelieving Gentiles say. Then in the eyes of the Christians, Christ is greater and higher. I am not saying that the Lord Jesus is neither great nor high. However, you have to realize that this notion is according to man's religious concept. Since the creation of man, God has always revealed Himself to man and placed Himself before man as the tree of life. We all know that fruit trees are not gigantic trees. For example, neither apple trees nor vines are tall. However, trees such as fir and cypress, which are used for pillars, are very tall. If the fruit trees were several hundred feet high with fruit hanging from them, at such a height how could we get the fruit to eat? Therefore, I firmly believe that the tree of life presented in the Bible must be a small and short tree. Some Bible scholars suggest that the tree of life is a grapevine because the Lord Jesus once declared, "I am the true vine." Regardless of this, the tree of life cannot be very tall or high.

Hallelujah, when God appeared to man the first time, He did not appear as a great One but rather as a tree placed before man! Then when Jesus came, men regarded Him as a tremendously great religious person. However, He said, "I am the bread of life." Bread is even smaller than a tree. God has always placed Himself before men as a small One; He never manifested Himself as a great One. Why? It is because only by being small can He enter into man. When we take Him into us, He is delighted.

Many of you are very familiar with Paul's Epistles. Let me ask you, "In Paul's fourteen Epistles, how many times did he write that he bowed his head and prostrated himself before God?" There are only a few instances. However, he repeatedly said, "Christ in me" and "Christ in you." For example, he said, "It is no longer I who live, but it is Christ who lives in me"; "It pleased God...to reveal His Son in me"; "My children, with whom I travail again in birth until Christ is formed in you"; "Christ in you, the hope of glory"; "That Christ may make His home in your hearts" (Gal. 2:20; 1:15-16; 4:19; Col. 1:27; Eph. 3:17). When something gets into you, which is greater, you or that thing? Hallelujah, you are greater! When you praise the Lord, you truly should tell Him, "Lord, I praise You, I am greater than You! O Lord, You are smaller than I!" If you dare not praise the Lord in this manner, it proves that you are still being influenced by your religious concepts. In the morning try to boldly say to the Lord, "Hallelujah! I am great, and You are small." If you do this, I can guarantee that your spirit will leap with joy. The Lord will then say, "Here is a man who knows Me thoroughly."

Do not misunderstand me. I am not saying that the Lord Jesus in His person is smaller than you. In Himself He is many times greater and higher than you are. However, He has indeed become a small Jesus in order that you may eat and enjoy Him. Moreover, when He left Jerusalem and withdrew to Tyre and Sidon, He became even the crumbs that fell under the table. The bread on the table is comparatively big; the crumbs under the table are truly small. "O Jesus, I praise You as the 'crumbs.' Today You are not a whole Jesus; You are Jesus as the 'crumbs!'"

About fifteen years ago in a long-term training here, I searched through the Bible and tried my best to find all the titles of the Lord. He is Christ, Jesus, Emmanuel, Son of God, and so on. We found about two hundred seventy titles. However, I did not include "the crumbs" as a title. This morning I want to add another title: The Lord Jesus is also called the crumbs. The Lord Jesus is not only the bread of life but also "the crumbs."

I repeat, Jesus in Himself is great, but in order for us to eat and enjoy Him, He willingly humbled Himself and took the form of a slave. Man, in his natural concept, called Him "the Son of David" which was a traditional form of address. However, the Lord Jesus said, "I am the children's bread, even the crumbs. I am not the crumbs on the table but rather the crumbs under the table." Oh, the Lord Jesus is in the place where you are—in a fallen condition, in Tyre and Sidon. Tyre and Sidon were not respectable places, yet the Lord withdrew to those places. Although He is holy, He humbled Himself and condescended to be with us, to approach the unrighteous sinners. As the great God, He approached the lowly men.

NOT MERELY ASKING THE LORD
TO DO THINGS FOR US, BUT EATING THE LORD

The Canaanite woman came to ask the Lord to do something for her. She begged the Lord to heal her sick daughter. However, the Lord's answer did not give any hint that He was going to do something. He said that He was the bread to feed her. By this we understand that we do not need the Lord Jesus to do anything for us; instead, we need to eat the Lord Jesus. Sisters, is your husband ill? Do not ask the Lord first to heal his sickness. The reason your husband is ill is so that you may eat the Lord Jesus. Take the Lord Jesus into you, and then your husband's illness will be healed. Are you vexed by your children's disobedience? You often pray that the Lord will perform a miracle to make your children obedient. However, the more you pray, the less effective your prayers are; the more you pray, the more disobedient your children are. Now you have to learn this secret: You have to eat the Lord more. Eat the Lord well, and your child will be healed.

Whenever you have a need, it is a proof that you need to eat the Lord Jesus. Have you lost your job? Do not pray to the Lord for a good job. All you need to do is eat the Lord Jesus, and the job will appear. When unbelievers hear these words, they will think that I am talking nonsense, but the experienced ones know that the job comes out of our eating the Lord. Do not ask the Lord Jesus to do something outside of you. Rather, eat the Lord Jesus and take Him into your being.

Brothers and sisters, we have all seen that the Lord Jesus has truly come to be our food. We need to change our concept. The elders in all the localities are faithfully managing the churches, bearing the churches on their hearts, and earnestly hoping that the churches will go on. Being anxious for the churches is good but not effective. Do not ask the Lord to help you take good care of the churches; you have to turn to take a few bites of the Lord Jesus. When you eat more of the Lord Jesus, the churches will be enlivened.

This is the central viewpoint in the New Testament. The Lord came not to work for us but to feed us. It is wrong to ask the Lord to till the ground for you like an ox; it is also wrong to shear the Lord of wool for your beauty. When the Canaanite woman in Matthew 15 asked the Lord Jesus to heal her sick daughter, the Lord replied in effect, "Do not ask Me to be an ox to till the ground for you; I am the crumbs for you to eat! Regardless of whether or not your daughter is sick, just eat Me! Eat Me, and your daughter will be healed!"

Brothers and sisters, your family life has problems because you do not eat Jesus. When the wives eat Jesus, the husbands change for the better; when the husbands eat Jesus, the wives change for the better. When the children eat Jesus, the parents no longer are a problem. When the parents eat the Lord Jesus, the children have a turn. You need to take the Lord Jesus into you and let Him become your life, your food, and your everything; then your circumstances will change. Actually, we do not care whether our circumstances are good or bad; we only care to eat and enjoy the Lord. The Lord is for you to eat! You first eat under the table, and then after a while you eat what is on the table. When the Gentile dogs eat Christ, they become the children of God. After the children eat more of Christ, they become the precious stones. In Revelation 2, the Lord told the messenger of the church in Pergamos, "To him who overcomes, to him I will give of the hidden manna, and to him I will give a white stone" (v. 17). The white stone is the one who overcomes. The one who eats the hidden manna eventually becomes the white stone for God's building.

THE THOUGHT IN THE BIBLE BEING TO EAT

When the prodigal son returned home, outwardly he was clothed with the best robe prepared by his father, but inwardly he was still hungry. Therefore, the father said, "Bring the fattened calf; slaughter it, and let us eat and be merry" (Luke 15:23). This is the thought in the New Testament as well as in the whole Bible.

The Lord Jesus also said that the preaching of the gospel is likened to a man preparing a great dinner. When we preach the gospel, we often tell people to repent and frequently speak about man being sinful. However, in this parable the Lord Jesus said, "Go and invite the guests! The dinner has been made. Come, for all things are now ready!" Come to do what? Come to eat! Do not worry that the unbelievers will fail to confess and repent of their sins. When they eat the Lord, they will rejoice. Later when they realize that they are sinful, they will weep. Such weeping and confessing of sins are better than what they would do after listening to your persuasion. Therefore, when we preach the gospel to others, we have to urge them to eat. Man needs to eat the Lord, to take the Lord in.

Paul said in his Epistles that he fed the believers with milk. Peter also said that as newborn babes we should long for the guileless, spiritual milk. Milk is not only for drinking but also for eating. Milk is nourishing food. Thus, the thought of the Bible is eating! The Bible is a book on eating! Eat! Eat! We need to eat the Lord Jesus!

CHAPTER THREE

COMING TO THE FEAST
AND KEEPING THE FEAST

Scripture Reading: Matt. 22:2-4; 1 Cor. 10:17-21; 11:23; 5:7-8; Rev. 3:20-21; 19:7-9

TO RECEIVE THE GOSPEL
BEING TO COME TO THE FEAST

In the New Testament we see that in His salvation the Lord pays attention to the matter of eating. The verses above show us that the gospel is a great feast. To be invited to a feast is to be asked to come and enjoy. I truly wish that you would read and pray over these verses again and again; then you will see that if this matter of eating were not so important, it would not be repeated over and over again in the New Testament. It is mentioned in Matthew, then in 1 Corinthians, and finally in Revelation. In God's view, His gospel is not focused on asking people to repent or to believe; even more it is not focused on asking them to join a religion. Rather, it is focused on inviting people to the feast. To come to the feast means to come and enjoy the Lord Jesus.

However, our natural concepts are too far off from this fact. If it were not for the fact that this matter is recorded in the Bible, we would never have this concept in our natural thinking. We would think that to receive the gospel is to repent, to believe, and to receive the truth. Actually, these things are still not the receiving of the gospel. To receive the gospel is to receive the Lord into us that we may eat, drink, and enjoy Him.

THE CHRISTIAN LIFE

In the New Testament the word *feast* is carried over from

the Old Testament in 1 Corinthians 5: "Let us keep the feast" (v. 8). In the Old Testament time God wanted His people to keep the feasts. That was only a type which has now been fulfilled in the New Testament. The fulfillment is that we enjoy the Lord Jesus. Our whole Christian life is a life of keeping the feast. Every day we are keeping the feast. Whenever we come to meet, we are keeping the feast. Every time we come together, whether we sing, pray-read, fellowship, exhort one another, supply one another, speak to one another, or listen to one another, the basic principle is that we are keeping the feast.

In the Gospel of Matthew the Lord said that the kingdom of the heavens is likened to a king who prepared a wedding feast for his son and who sent his slaves to ask the invited ones to come to the feast (22:2-4). Then at the end of Revelation, it says, "The marriage of the Lamb has come....Blessed are they who are called to the marriage dinner of the Lamb" (19:7, 9). We see from this that the New Testament begins with a feast, and it also ends with a feast. What are you doing here today? If you say that you came to attend the conference, that is not so good. If you say that you came to attend a worship service, that is even worse. What did you come here for? To attend a feast! Whose feast is it? It is the marriage feast of the Lamb! We come not only to a feast but even to a wedding feast. This feast of great joy is the marriage feast of Christ. Do you know when this feast began? It began on the day of Pentecost, a short time after the Lord Jesus ascended to the heavens. This marriage feast lasts not only for two hours or two days. It began with Pentecost, and it is still going on today.

The messages we previously heard when we were in Christianity were mostly under the influence of natural concepts. Consider what the first thing in your mind was after you were saved. Immediately after we were saved, some of us had the notion that from now on we must go to more meetings, learn and understand more truths, pay more attention to the Bible, and other things of this nature. Is there one who, after he was saved, joyfully said that he was invited to a feast and that he is attending the marriage feast of the Lamb? I do not believe that we can find such a Christian. However, the Lord's word tells us clearly that to be saved is to be invited to a feast. In the universe God has prepared a great wedding feast for His Son. God said, "Come! All things are ready."

We have to realize that the heavens and the earth are a great wedding chamber. The whole universe is the story of a marriage feast. No matter how much trouble the devil is creating, how vile sins are on the earth, how corrupt the human race is, and how evil the human heart is, these are only the dark side. Every item has two sides—a white side and a black side, a bright side and a dark side, a happy side and a sad side. People on the earth see the dark side and the sad side of things, but God in the heavens sees the bright side and the happy side. The more we look at the situation on earth, the sadder we feel because the world is becoming worse and worse. However, God is happy as He watches in heaven. God says, "My Son has a wedding chamber, and I am preparing a marriage feast for My Son. I do not care that the people on earth are making trouble. I want to invite them to the feast. Come! All things are ready!"

We are delivered from the world not by gnashing our teeth nor by listening to sermons nor by being exhorted nor by being regulated; we are delivered from the world by being fed with Christ. When we have tasted Christ and have eaten Him to the full, we no longer want the world even if others offer it to us. Let the others be busy with the world; that is not our business. Our business is to attend the feast every day, to eat Christ and enjoy Christ day by day. Therefore, Paul said that we are keeping the feast.

How do we keep the feast? We keep the feast by eating the unleavened bread of sincerity and truth. In this unleavened bread there are all kinds of elements, such as love, truth, enlightenment, holiness, power, and patience. This unleavened bread of sincerity and truth is Christ. We keep the feast not by learning the truths and listening to messages but altogether by eating Christ. The more we eat Christ, the more we have His elements.

God does not have any intention for us to labor or to struggle or to strive. It is true that the Bible says, "The kingdom of

the heavens is taken by violence" (Matt. 11:12), but this word
implies that we need to enjoy Christ in our spirit. The entire
New Testament age is not an age of labor but a great feast.
Remember that in the Old Testament type one was not
allowed to labor during the feasts. In the regular days everyone had to labor. However, during the feasts, no one was
allowed to labor; rather, everyone simply ate, drank, and
enjoyed. Moreover, during the feasts, they did not eat poorly;
rather, they ate the good things, and they feasted.

THE BREAKING OF BREAD MEETING
BEING THE LORD'S FEAST

Why do we have the breaking of bread meeting frequently?
What does it mean to break the bread? Notice the phrase in
1 Corinthians 10:21, *the Lord's table.* The breaking of bread
meeting is our coming to the Lord's table, the Lord's feast. At
this table, in this feast, we eat the Lord's body and drink the
Lord's blood. In other words, we eat and drink the Lord. At
the same time, when we break the bread, we also declare and
testify to the whole universe that we are a group of Christians
who live a life of daily feasting on Christ, daily eating Christ,
and daily enjoying Christ. Whenever we break the bread, it is
an exhibition of our daily life. In our normal living we eat the
Lord, drink the Lord, and enjoy the Lord. Then on the Lord's
Day we come together to have an exhibition for everyone, for
all creation to see, declaring to them that our life is a life of
enjoying the Lord.

Brothers, in our Lord's table meetings in the past, we still
held some traditional concepts in paying attention to how
to praise the Lord and how to worship the Father. We learned
these things from the Brethren. Although these things are
not wrong, they are merely traditional. Actually, the important thing at the Lord's table is not whether to praise or not
to praise. Rather, it is to open up our spirit and exhibit once
again for the angels and Satan to see how we receive Christ
into us. At that time we may praise or not praise.

I believe that the Brethren truly saw the light, yet the
light they saw was still limited by natural human concepts.
Therefore, we cannot take that way any longer. If we continue

following the old way of the Brethren, our spirit will become lame. Therefore, the emphasis of the Lord's table is once again on opening ourselves to receive and enjoy the Lord!

For example, two brothers may come to the Lord's table. One of them is a well-behaved, good brother. Before he comes to the meeting, he examines himself to see if he has offended anyone or if he has committed any sin. After he sits down in the meeting hall, he behaves properly and strictly. When others sing, he sings along; when others pray, he says amen; when the bread is passed to him, he takes a piece; when the cup is passed to him, he drinks a little. He also praises the Lord and worships the Father. However, there is not a bit of change in him. When he leaves, he is the same as when he came in. However, it may not be so with the other brother. This second brother may be one who is usually quite naughty and mischievous, and he may have had a big quarrel with somebody the previous day. However, when he comes to break the bread, he touches the Spirit, and he opens himself completely. He does not care for praising or not praising, but he once again simply receives the Lord at the Lord's table. When he receives the Lord, his whole being turns, and he shouts, "Hallelujah!" At that moment he is soaring to the clouds. There is no need for you to talk to him about sins or about the things on earth. There is no dust in the clouds. If you tell him not to lose his temper with others, you bring him down from the cloud. Once he opens up from within and receives the Lord, he soars to the skies. On the other hand, the well-behaved brother is like a crawling insect on earth; he is still climbing the mountain. This is the difference between one who enjoys Christ and one who does not.

Forgive me for saying this. Some among you may have been coming to the Lord's table meeting every Lord's Day for eighteen years already, and you are still a well-behaved "crawling insect." You have been a Christian for eighteen years and have always behaved properly. Your wife says that you are very good, and your friends say that you are good-natured. No one criticizes you, yet you remain a crawling insect on earth. Everyone falls, but you never fall. You just keep crawling, slowly and steadily.

Someone may have been naughty before, yet in one of the meetings he touches the Lord. After he has touched the Lord, he comes again the next Lord's Day to touch the Lord. He does not come to receive the so-called Holy Communion or to behave himself or to worship the Father. He comes simply to touch the Lord. He is like a 747 jumbo jet stopping to refuel when the fuel runs low. The Lord's table is his refueling station. After being fueled up, this brother can run for another week, and then he returns the next week to refuel.

Therefore, to come to the Lord's table is to come to a feast, and it is also to come to refuel. It is not a matter of receiving outward teachings, outward corrections, or outward exhortations; instead, it is a matter of meeting the Lord inwardly. Thus, our meeting does not need any regulation. What is the use of regulations? What is their value? It is good enough to touch the Lord within. As long as we are fueled up within, it is not a matter of whether we behave or we do not behave, whether we shout, roll on the floor, or jump; everything will be all right.

However, I do not encourage you to invent some gimmicks; that would be meaningless. To be clever is one thing, but to touch the Lord is another. We do not want regulations because we do not want them to limit people from touching the Lord. However, if we turn this liberty into engaging in gimmicks, that is meaningless. The important thing is that you are not bound, but rather that your whole being is open, free, and released so that you have easy access to the Lord.

Since the Lord's table is a declaration, this declaration must have the life as its backing. If your private life is not the same as what you declare, then what you do at the meeting is not a declaration but a performance, a show. If your private life is not a life of enjoying Christ and you come just to perform at the meeting, that is false. Our Lord's table is not a performance or a show; it is a testimony, a declaration, telling the whole universe that this is the way we live. We daily eat the Lord, drink the Lord, and enjoy the Lord; therefore, we now come together to testify to the whole universe that we are a group of people who eat, drink, and enjoy the Lord.

Now I believe that when you come again to the Lord's table, your concept will be changed. You will not come to keep any regulation. In fact, there is no need to keep any regulation. Your spirit is open, and you contact the Lord and touch the Lord in your spirit. There is no regulation or restriction upon you. This is the way you live every day—without rituals or regulations but opening to the Lord in your spirit to eat and drink Him continually. Then when the Lord's Day comes, we all come together to make a declaration once again that this is the way we spend our days. We keep the feast every day. How long should we keep the feast? The Lord Jesus told us we should do this "until that day when I drink it new with you" (Matt. 26:29). One day we will feast with Him face to face. Today we start feasting until the day when we will dine at the new feast.

THE CHURCH BECOMING DEGRADED
BECAUSE OF NOT ENJOYING THE LORD

Look at the degradation of the churches in Ephesus and in Laodicea. They became degraded in that they fell away from the enjoyment of the Lord. They merely worked and labored and paid attention to doctrines and teachings. They degraded to such an extent that even though they knew and understood all the doctrines, the Lord seemed to say, "Since you are neither hot nor cold, you have been removed from My feast. I am outside your door knocking. You need to open up yourself to Me that I may come in to you and dine with you and you with Me. You were at the feast when you were first saved, but you abandoned the feast and fell into degraded Christianity. I am calling you to be an overcomer and to be delivered from the condition of not feasting. Open yourself and let Me come into you so that you and I may feast together." This feast will continue until the marriage feast of the Lamb in Revelation 19. At that time blessed will be those who are invited to the feast. Hallelujah!

CHAPTER FOUR

TWO KINDS OF EATING—EATING IN SOWING AND EATING IN HARVESTING

Scripture Reading: Deut. 12:5-9, 17-18; 14:22-23; 15:19-21; 16:9-10, 13-17

We thank the Lord that now we all are learning to eat the Lord. However, according to the revelation in Deuteronomy, there are many particular points in the matter of eating, drinking, and enjoying the Lord. On the one hand, the Lord is the bread of life, and we simply need to eat Him. On the other hand, according to Deuteronomy 12, 14, and 15, the Lord Jesus, whom we eat, comes out of our laboring; He is produced from our sowing of the field and from our raising of the herd and the flock. Therefore, according to Deuteronomy, our enjoyment of the riches of the Lord is the result of our laboring on Him.

I can further describe the particulars of this type of eating. For example, if you open your Bible, call on the name of the Lord, and pray-read His word, you can enjoy the Lord even now. However, this is only the initial enjoyment; it is not the enjoyment of a rich harvest, because it is devoid of your own toil and labor. You enjoy the Lord simply by opening up yourself, by using your spirit to call on His name, and by pray-reading His Word. This is the enjoyment in sowing but not the enjoyment in harvesting.

Many of you have testified regarding your enjoyment of the Lord, but all that I have heard pertains to your eating, your enjoyment in sowing. You have not yet reached the level of eating with regard to harvesting. The initial sowing is easy, but the final harvesting is not so easy. After the seeds are sown, whether or not there will be a harvest is still a

question. Up until now, your eating of the Lord for enjoyment
has been in the initial stage, the sowing stage.

Therefore, I have to make it clear to you, brothers and
sisters, that you should not stop at the enjoyment of sowing,
but go on to the enjoyment of harvesting. When you sow, you
simply bury the seed into the ground. After sowing, you still
need to take care of the sprout that it may grow and bear
fruit. Only then can you have the enjoyment of the harvest. In
our enjoyment of sowing, we receive something of the Lord
into us. Whenever we call on the name of the Lord and
pray-read His word, we receive a portion of the Lord as a seed
into us. Whether this will result in a harvest depends upon
our willingness to let the seed grow. If we let it grow, it will
surely yield a harvest. Otherwise, nothing will happen.

NEEDING TO LABOR FOR A RICH HARVEST

According to my own observation, the enjoyment of the
brothers and sisters is mostly in the enjoyment of sowing.
Most of the seeds that are sown into you have no result. Why
is there no result? This is because after you eat, drink, and
enjoy the Lord, you do not let Him grow, mature, and bear
fruit in you.

Suppose you call, "O Lord Jesus." I believe that this calling
will have a definite effect on you. You cannot call on the Lord
without any consequence. He comes to you whenever you call
on Him. On the one hand, He will come to comfort you; on the
other hand, He might come to bother you. If you as a husband
call, "O Lord! O Lord!", He may come to touch you within,
saying, "See? You have offended your wife." You may say,
"O Lord! Cleanse me with Your precious blood!" But He may
go on to say, "Indeed, the blood can cleanse you, but it cannot
confess your sins for you. Go quickly and confess to your
wife!" What should you do? Some husbands may harden their
hearts and refuse to obey. Because they refuse to turn, the
Lord is through with them. If you were such a one and you
tried again to call, "O Lord," it would not be as effective as
before. The Lord Jesus knows your story; therefore, when you
call on Him again, He will not move. We all have had this kind
of experience. In the past He came when you called, "O Lord";

now He does not come. The more you call, the less it works; the more you say "O..." the more deflated you are. Then you may begin to question the practice of calling on the name of the Lord to such an extent that you do not want to call any longer. Is this not pitiful? You only sow the seed into the ground, but you do not let the seed grow to have a harvest. Eventually, even the enjoyment of the seed is gone.

Isaiah 55:10 says, "That it may give seed to the sower and bread to the eater." I sow a seed into the ground, and it yields thirty seeds; I consume fifteen of them and still have fifteen seeds to sow for the next year. But what is your situation? The seed you have sown is finished because it did not grow. Therefore, there are no more seeds. Why are you out of seeds? It is because you did not let the seed grow.

When you call, "O Lord," and the Lord gives you a sense that you have offended your wife, if you would quickly confess your sins before the Lord and also go to your wife to admit your failure and ask her for forgiveness, then the seed in you will grow very fast. When you come back to call, "O Lord," the flavor is completely different. However, the Lord keeps on bothering you. When you call, "O Lord" again, He comes to point out that your hair is not cut properly and that you have to take care of this matter. If you obey immediately and get a proper haircut, you will sense much joy in you. Dear brothers and sisters, when this is the case, the result is tremendous. Your inner being becomes a field, a big farm, that has a rich reaping every day. This truly fulfills the word spoken by Isaiah, to give seed to the sower and bread to the eater. Today I want to check with you all. Do you as sowers truly have seeds? Do you as eaters really have bread? Perhaps you have only half a bowl of rice, which is not enough even for yourself. If you cannot feed yourself adequately, how will you be able to take care of others? What is the reason for this? It is because you sow the seed, yet you do not labor to let the seed grow.

We all know that when a farmer labors on a field, he has to remove the stones, eliminate the weeds, water the soil, add fertilizer, and sometimes apply some pesticides. What do you do? You have done very well eating the Lord and pray-reading

His word, but you do not remove the stones, nor eliminate the weeds, nor water the soil, nor add fertilizer, nor apply pesticides. In the end you might as well have not sown at all. If you do not sow, your seeds will remain intact, but once you sow, you lose the only seeds you have. There are some people who indeed have a reserve of a small portion of the Lord before pray-reading the Word, but after they gained the Lord through pray-reading and then are disobedient by not laboring, they lose the presence of the Lord. The Lord went farther away from them.

A COMPARISON BETWEEN MANNA
AND THE PRODUCE OF CANAAN

In Deuteronomy laboring on the land of Canaan was altogether different from gathering manna in the wilderness. Indeed, the land of Canaan was God-given, the seeds were God-given, and the necessary things, such as the air, the sunshine, and the rain were all given by God. However, in addition to these gifts, the people still needed to labor. If they did not labor on the field, the Lord could not do anything. In typology the seeds, the sunlight, the rain, and even the physical strength the people had with which to sow and labor on the land, all were the Lord Himself. Nevertheless, their cooperation with the Lord was required. They could not reap the produce of the land unless they cooperated. The produce of the land is different from the manna. Manna was given purely from heaven. There was no need for man to sow, reap, or cooperate with God. Of course, in order to have the manna to eat, one still had to go out and gather it early in the morning. If someone were lazy and went out late, there would be nothing to gather. Yes, this going out in the morning may be considered cooperation, but this was a minimal amount of cooperation. To gain the produce of the land was entirely different. To gain the produce of the land required the people's cooperation from the beginning to the end. God gave the water, sunshine, air, and seeds. However, God would not labor for them; they had to do their own laboring.

Let me ask you this: Which is better and higher, manna or the produce of the good land of Canaan? Naturally, you will say that the produce of the land of Canaan is superior. In what way is it superior? First, the produce is for offering. The manna that descends from heaven is good in the eyes of man, but God does not want manna as an offering. God did not say that we should offer manna as a burnt offering, a wave offering, or a heave offering. Rather, He said, "Eat! It is only good to be your food; it is not good enough to be My offering." Manna does not qualify as an offering. Offerings are for the worship of God. Manna is good, but it does not qualify to be used in the worship of God. If you want to worship God, you have to bring the produce of the good land of Canaan; only the produce of the good land can constitute your worship to God. Regardless of how much manna you eat, as in the case of the people of Israel who ate manna for forty years, it is not sufficient to constitute your worship to God. You have to eat the produce of the land of Canaan; only this produce can constitute your worship to God. Therefore, by this you see that manna is inferior, whereas the produce of the land of Canaan is superior.

Let me ask you, brothers and sisters, what do you eat today, manna or the produce of the good land? Some say they eat manna; others say they eat manna as well as the produce. This is true. However, I hope that those who eat manna will gradually stop eating it. Do you know where manna was eaten? It was eaten in the wilderness. Therefore, eating manna is a strong proof that you are a wanderer. Where was the produce of the good land eaten? It was eaten in Canaan! Moreover, the top tenth of the harvest of the land—the first-born of the herd and of the flock and the firstfruits of the grain—were not to be eaten at home. They had to be brought to the temple and eaten before God. This shows that their wandering had ceased.

Do you want to be a Christian who eats manna or a Christian who eats the produce of the good land? Everyone wants to be a Christian who eats the produce of the good land. True, manna is good; but it is not good enough because it is the diet of those who wander about in the wilderness. Joshua 5 shows clearly that the manna ceased to descend from heaven immediately after the children of Israel entered into Canaan and began to eat the produce of the land (v. 12). Once you have eaten the produce of the good land, you do not need manna anymore because you experience something deeper and enjoy something better. Henceforth, we have to exercise not to eat manna anymore. Yes, manna is Christ, but it is Christ as our supply during our wandering days. We need to enter into the land of Canaan, where the produce is far better than manna.

ACCEPTING THE DEALINGS IN OUR LIFE TO HAVE A RICH HARVEST

To obtain manna does not require our laboring, but to get the produce of the land of Canaan does. While we are enjoying the Lord and receiving Him into us, He often raises up circumstances and allows many things to happen for our good, so that the seed in us can grow and produce something. For example, a sister, whose husband always makes things difficult for her, prays every day, asking the Lord to cause her husband to love Him as much as she does. However, the more she prays, the less he loves the Lord; the more she calls "O Lord, Amen!" and the more she pray-reads, the more her husband is annoyed. Previously, her husband attended two meetings a week; after her calling and pray-reading, her husband would not go even for half a meeting. In a case like this what should you do? Let me tell you that all those things that happen are the Lord's raising up the north wind to blow upon you (S. S. 4:16). Instead of asking the Lord to change your husband, pray that the Lord will grow in you: "O Lord, make me willing to accept Your dealing. O Lord, subdue me from within. O Lord, cause me to submit myself under Your hand and take the breaking." Later you will thank and praise the Lord that because you were willing to be dealt with in that way, the life in you grew a little.

You may begin to feel good about dealings such as these when the life in you grows a little today and a little more tomorrow. However, on the third day even your children may take sides with their father and begin to help him to deal with you. What should you do? This is again the blowing of the north wind to deal with you. You have to learn to accept it.

Do you know that once you accept the dealing and call on the Lord again, the taste will become so wonderful? Whenever you call on Him, He comes. Then there is a harvest in you. Thus, you have an abundant supply of seeds to sow and of bread to eat. At the same time you can bring the top tenth, the firstfruits, of the produce to the meetings to eat and enjoy with the saints. This eating is your worship. This is what is lacking in Christianity and even in our midst. However, the Lord wants to recover this. Without recovering this, it is difficult for the church to mature, for the bride to be made ready, and for the Lord to return. Therefore, this matter is crucial.

LABORING ON CHRIST AND THE CHURCH LIFE

Brothers and sisters, I have the full assurance that this is what the Lord is recovering today. The Lord is not recovering your small virtue, your small victory, or your small holiness. What the Lord wants is a group of people who enter into His Word and into His eternal plan. This is not a matter of restraining yourself from losing your temper, a matter of being victorious, or a matter of being holy. Rather, it is a matter of touching the Lord in a real way and of allowing Him to grow and mature in you. When you have an abundant harvest, you have enough not only to feed yourself but also for inviting brothers and sisters to eat with you. Moreover, you will have the topmost portion that could be brought to the meetings to offer to God. This is the genuine church life. In the meeting you testify Christ, and I also testify Christ. We all offer Christ before God, and we enjoy Christ together with the brothers and sisters after God has been satisfied. This is the church meeting. This is our worship and the practical living and testimony of the church.

I truly feel that in what we saw formerly concerning the testimony of the church and the church being the expression of Christ, there were more or less some natural elements; we did not thoroughly see these matters of eating and growing. Twenty years ago, when I saw brothers who had good character and proper behavior and who gave good impressions wherever they went, I greatly appreciated them. However, now in retrospect those brothers with good character and proper behavior did not bear any good fruit. On the contrary, some careless and sloppy ones were able to bring people to salvation. The church life, the testimony of the church, is not a matter of behaving well or not behaving well, nor is it a matter of being or not being above reproach. The church life, the testimony of the church, is a matter of eating the Lord as the seed and allowing this seed to grow. Like a farmer, you remove the stones, eliminate the weeds, water the ground, add fertilizer, and apply pesticides so that the Christ in you will gradually grow into a harvest. This is not a matter of being well-behaved or not; it is a matter in a totally different realm. Behaving and not behaving are in the realm of good and evil. What we are speaking about is the realm of Christ. You are full of Christ, and you bring in your topmost portion before God to enjoy with the saints in the meeting. This is our proper meeting today. The emphasis in the meeting is not on singing, praying, praising, speaking in tongues, or functioning; the emphasis is on bringing in the topmost portion of the Christ that you have produced. I bring my portion, and you bring yours. Apart from any forms, we all present our Christ.

TAKING HEED TO LABOR

I feel that the great lack we have today in the matter of bringing Christ to the meetings is that our harvest is not rich. This is why sometimes when you come to testify, you try to use some gimmicks. I am not saying that you should refrain from all kinds of methods, but I am afraid that you have these without content. The gimmicks are for embellishment; they are not the content. I would prefer not to have any gimmicks or methods but rather to have more content. We cannot gain substance in our testimonies in only a few days; we need to labor for an extended period of time.

Brothers and sisters, we have to turn back to the Lord to have a harvest. We have to labor that we may grow something. Sometimes the Lord is like the grain sown into us; at other times He is in us as a small tree. This tree may be an olive tree, a vine, a fig tree, or a pomegranate tree. You need to cultivate it that it may grow and bear fruit. Then when you come to the meetings, you will have the firstfruit to offer to God.

The problem today is that when we come to the meetings, we only know how to release our spirit and call on the name of the Lord; we cannot present anything with substance to enjoy with others. This may be likened to coming to the feast empty-handed or with only a small pigeon, which is enough for only one meal. Since many are devoid of things to present, they have to resort to some amusing activities to make people laugh. Regrettably, everyone then remains empty within.

If we have an abundant harvest and are rich in grain, new wine, bulls, sheep, and pigeons, we can bring in our produce, basket upon basket and pile upon pile. We can present our bulls, sheep, pigeons, and fruit. That will be very rich. Everyone will be very supplied and will want to come back the next time.

I hope you will not spend your energy on gimmicks; rather, you will use your effort to produce a content. You need to sow the field, cultivate the fruit trees, tend the cattle, and take care of the pigeons. Subsequently, the crops in the field, the trees on the mountains, the bulls, sheep, and pigeons on the farm will all grow. You will be rich because everything in you will be continually growing. By this way the sower has seed, the eater has bread, and the offerer has something to offer. When everyone brings his riches to the meetings, the meetings will be delivered from all the old ways.

I have this much to say at this time. Now we all have learned to eat. We have learned that there are two kinds of eating. One is the eating in sowing, and the other is the eating in harvesting. The eating in sowing cannot constitute our worship; we need the eating in harvesting. When you bring the eating in harvesting, that will constitute the true worship and the genuine church life. The church needs this. We have to look to the Lord and open up to Him that we all may learn to be exercised in the matter of eating.

ABOUT THE AUTHOR

Witness Lee was born in 1905 in northern China and raised in a Christian family. At age 19 he was fully captured for Christ and immediately consecrated himself to preach the gospel for the rest of his life. Early in his service, he met Watchman Nee, a renowned preacher, teacher, and writer. Witness Lee labored together with Watchman Nee under his direction. In 1934 Watchman Nee entrusted Witness Lee with the responsibility for his publication operation, called the Shanghai Gospel Bookroom.

Prior to the Communist takeover in 1949, Witness Lee was sent by Watchman Nee and his other co-workers to Taiwan to insure that the things delivered to them by the Lord would not be lost. Watchman Nee instructed Witness Lee to continue the former's publishing operation abroad as the Taiwan Gospel Bookroom, which has been publicly recognized as the publisher of Watchman Nee's works outside China. Witness Lee's work in Taiwan manifested the Lord's abundant blessing. From a mere 350 believers, newly fled from the mainland, the churches in Taiwan grew to 20,000 in five years.

In 1962 Witness Lee felt led of the Lord to come to the United States, settling in California. During his 35 years of service in the U.S., he ministered in weekly meetings and weekend conferences, delivering several thousand spoken messages. Much of his speaking has since been published as over 400 titles. Many of these have been translated into over fourteen languages. He gave his last public conference in February 1997 at the age of 91.

He leaves behind a prolific presentation of the truth in the Bible. His major work, *Life-study of the Bible,* comprises over 25,000 pages of commentary on every book of the Bible from the perspective of the believers' enjoyment and experience of God's divine life in Christ through the Holy Spirit. Witness Lee was the chief editor of a new translation of the New Testament into Chinese called the Recovery Version and directed the translation of the same into English. The Recovery Version also appears in a number of other languages. He provided an extensive body of footnotes, outlines, and spiritual cross references. A radio broadcast of his messages can be heard on Christian radio stations in the United States. In 1965 Witness Lee founded Living Stream Ministry, a non-profit corporation, located in Anaheim, California, which officially presents his and Watchman Nee's ministry.

Witness Lee's ministry emphasizes the experience of Christ as life and the practical oneness of the believers as the Body of Christ. Stressing the importance of attending to both these matters, he led the churches under his care to grow in Christian life and function. He was unbending in his conviction that God's goal is not narrow sectarianism but the Body of Christ. In time, believers began to meet simply as the church in their localities in response to this conviction. In recent years a number of new churches have been raised up in Russia and in many eastern European countries.

OTHER BOOKS PUBLISHED BY
Living Stream Ministry

Titles by Witness Lee:

Abraham—Called by God	0-7363-0359-6
The Experience of Life	0-87083-417-7
The Knowledge of Life	0-87083-419-3
The Tree of Life	0-87083-300-6
The Economy of God	0-87083-415-0
The Divine Economy	0-87083-268-9
God's New Testament Economy	0-87083-199-2
The World Situation and God's Move	0-87083-092-9
Christ vs. Religion	0-87083-010-4
The All-inclusive Christ	0-87083-020-1
Gospel Outlines	0-87083-039-2
Character	0-87083-322-7
The Secret of Experiencing Christ	0-87083-227-1
The Life and Way for the Practice of the Church Life	0-87083-785-0
The Basic Revelation in the Holy Scriptures	0-87083-105-4
The Crucial Revelation of Life in the Scriptures	0-87083-372-3
The Spirit with Our Spirit	0-87083-798-2
Christ as the Reality	0-87083-047-3
The Central Line of the Divine Revelation	0-87083-960-8
The Full Knowledge of the Word of God	0-87083-289-1
Watchman Nee—A Seer of the Divine Revelation ...	0-87083-625-0

Titles by Watchman Nee:

How to Study the Bible	0-7363-0407-X
God's Overcomers	0-7363-0433-9
The New Covenant	0-7363-0088-0
The Spiritual Man 3 volumes	0-7363-0269-7
Authority and Submission	0-7363-0185-2
The Overcoming Life	1-57593-817-0
The Glorious Church	0-87083-745-1
The Prayer Ministry of the Church	0-87083-860-1
The Breaking of the Outer Man and the Release ...	1-57593-955-X
The Mystery of Christ	1-57593-954-1
The God of Abraham, Isaac, and Jacob	0-87083-932-2
The Song of Songs	0-87083-872-5
The Gospel of God 2 volumes	1-57593-953-3
The Normal Christian Church Life	0-87083-027-9
The Character of the Lord's Worker	1-57593-322-5
The Normal Christian Faith	0-87083-748-6
Watchman Nee's Testimony	0-87083-051-1

Available at
Christian bookstores, or contact Living Stream Ministry
2431 W. La Palma Ave. • Anaheim, CA 92801
1-800-549-5164 • www.livingstream.com